Dennis O'Driscoll

WEATHER PERMITTING

ANVIL PRESS POETRY

Published in 1999
by Anvil Press Poetry Ltd
Neptune House 70 Royal Hill London SE10 8RF
www.anvilpresspoetry.com

Reprinted in 2000, 2001

This book is published with financial assistance
from The Arts Council of England

Designed and set in Ehrhardt by Anvil
Printed and bound in England
by Cromwell Press, Trowbridge, Wiltshire

ISBN 0 85646 315 9

A catalogue record for this book
is available from the British Library

JULIE
through thick and thin

ACKNOWLEDGEMENTS

Thanks are due to the editors of the following publications in which some of the poems in this collection first appeared: *Agenda, Céide, College Green, The Irish Times, London Magazine, New England Review, Nocturnal Submissions, The North, Poetry Ireland Review, Poetry Review, Princeton University Library Chronicle, Quadrant, The Sunday Times, Thumbscrew, The Yale Review*; also to the editors of the anthologies *At the Year's Turning* (Dedalus), *Poetry Now* (Dun Laoghaire Rathdown) and *Scanning the Century* (Penguin). 'Tomorrow' was published in *Poetry* (Chicago).

CONTENTS

Part One

Part Two

Part Three

PART ONE

EITHER

They are somewhere in the world, pouring soya milk
on porridge during the dream-time before work,
     or sprouting thick fungal whiskers
     in a graveyard's penetrating damp –
the ones I used to know, with whom I lost
touch, who were once the mainstay of my
     gossip: squash partners, office colleagues,
     obnoxious neighbours, friends of friends.

As I speak, they scrutinise the milk carton's text
or subside more comfortably into the sleep
     that resurrection's long-haul wait entails.
     Our paths crossed, then grassed over again.
They are either alive and well or decomposing
slowly in a shroud; I could either call them up
     and chat, or confirm that they are ex-directory now.
     It is a matter of life or death.

FOUR DESTINATIONS

You travel under
cover of darkness

that lifts for the length
of a one-street village,

a hill farm scoured
by yard light.

Then night comes
down again in sheets.

You feel tired and cold,
a fire inhaling its own ash.

*

Why, as soon as the unaccompanied
cello suite begins, am I conveyed back
to the brittle wintry airport road,
your newly-widowed mother driving,
my arrival coinciding with a glacial
dusk, with the one customer left
to moderate the plate glass expanse
of an Arby's Sandwich franchise?

*

Regret is the hamlet across the bay
against which waves beat their brains
in winter, having lost all hope of change.

A door bangs. A cigarette sign swings
from rusty hinges. A slow piano theme
is rehearsed like an excuse.

*

As the Friday-evening bus speeds from the city,
moonlight restores wildness to the fields.
We place our fate in the driver's hands,
having offered up our fares, hearts,
spinal cords, endocrinal glands.

BACKGROUND MUSIC

It is not music you are listening to, it is not
your song they are playing, but the time outdoors
those same chords struck: Mahler's hammer blows fell
as dusk crashed down like cymbals on the perspex
shell where the orchestra was pitted against
birdsong, the sky's membrane raised like a roof.

It is not the melody but the warm air it drifts on,
through a window open to let paint dry, a daughter
prying the piano keys for notes in the dull acoustics
of an immaculate white room; or a string quartet silhouetted
before a curving bay: you have travelled east into a second
spring, rays cascading through an ice-melt of blue glass.

And that pop-song: ignore the ear-rotting, saccharine words;
let it transport you back to school holidays, cycling
torpid afternoons away, circling the oblong square.
Stuccoed houses in a Mitteleuropa city, a Sunday heavy with dust
of ribboned war wreaths, history; dark-eyed surveillance
from backstreet bars, a gypsy guitar wafting like nicotine.

A bugler's reveille from his campsite, dissipating river mist.
An organ fugue through incense after a cathedral Mass
at which the host clung to the cupola of your mouth.
Scratchy childhood tunes, loudhailed by a carnival, croon
through bloated heat; you try to sleep amid the corncrake-hoarse
excitement – cross-hatched sounds that fuse in memory now,

a Charles Ives symphony improvised on the spot.

THE CELTIC TIGER

Ireland's boom is in full swing.
Rows of numbers, set in a cloudless blue
computer background, prove the point.

Executives lop miles off journeys
since the ring-roads opened, one hand
free to dial a client on the mobile.

Outside new antique pubs, young consultants
– well-toned women, gel-slick men –
drain long-necked bottles of imported beer.

Lip-glossed cigarettes are poised
at coy angles, a black bra strap
slides strategically from a Rocha top.

Talk of tax-exempted town-house lettings
is muffled by rap music blasted
from a passing four-wheel drive.

The old live on, wait out their stay
of execution in small granny flats,
thrifty thin-lipped men, grim pious wives . . .

Sudden as an impulse holiday, the wind
has changed direction, strewing a whiff
of barbecue fuel across summer lawns.

Tonight, the babe on short-term
contract from the German parent
will partner you at the sponsors' concert.

Time now, however, for the lunch-break
orders to be faxed. Make yours hummus
on black olive bread. An Evian.

JET AGE

Years, centuries, millennia will pass. Highways and airports
will be reclaimed by twitch grass or covered with sand.

— IVAN KLÍMA

The stories we will regale our grandchildren with,
aluminium whales plunging to within inches of our lives,
diving down on cities, capsules stacked above the tarmac
before wheezing to a breathless halt (where swaying grass
will replace windsocks, fuel trucks rust on apron cracks);

spread-eagled tonnage taking off, a magic carpet rising
on its dust, vapour trails like silver rails to glide along,
live cargo strapped to padded seats commanding sight of land
stranded in sea-water; clouds like rose-tipped corries,
exhausted quarries, frozen canyons, unconquered peaks . . .

So inured to mystery, we will say, they took for granted
sprayed glitter of night cities, towns riveted to the ground,
but stirred from newspaper or snooze to adjust their watches
and their headrests, choose a complimentary liqueur.

NOR

'There didn't have to be 2,000 diseases
of the skin,' I remember someone commenting.
Nor 17,293 painfully slow routes through the vomitory
before being thrown to the lions of death.
Nor 11,416 ways of feeling wounded.
Nor 89,010 gradations of loneliness
calibrated on traffic islands, country lanes.
Nor 29,109,352 reasons to toss and turn at night.
Nor stage fright, nor honeymoon cystitis.
Nor *esprit de l'escalier*, nor so many calories in cream.
Nor sexually transmitted fatalities, nor smoker's cough.
Nor 250,000,000 tons (live weight) of humanity
to experience these things, nor however many
newborn pounds were dragged screaming, added
to the tally, since my opening line.

IN MEMORY OF ALOIS ALZHEIMER
(1864–1915)

I

Before this page fades from memory,
spare a thought for Alois Alzheimer,
called to mind each time

someone becomes forgetful,
disintegration vindicating
his good name.

II

His is the last image assigned
to the ex-President who has slipped
from public view; soiled sheets
give credence to his thesis;

his territory is marked out
by the track of urine
dribbled along the corridor
of the day-care centre.

III

Lie closer to me in the dry sheets
while I can still tell who you are.

Let me declare how much I love you
before our bed is sorely tested.

Love me with drooling toxins, with carbon monoxide,
with rope, with arrows through my heart.

THE VICTIM

I

The victim is male.
In his early thirties.
That's all the police will reveal for now.
Relatives have yet to be informed.
A post-mortem has yet to be scheduled.
The coroner's beeper is sounding its alarm.
What faith, tribe, gang he subscribed to.
Whether he had been involved or not.
Whether it was a random killing.
Whether it was a revenge attack, a tit-for-tat.
Speculation can wait for tomorrow's papers.

II

Until he is given a life.
Until he is given an address, wife, children, job.
Until he is a man with a history, a past.
Until the mystery of his death is cleared up.
Until the blood is swabbed from his chin.
Until the mud is laundered from his clothes.
Until someone claims his body
for family or nation or God.
Until guilt, forgiveness, innocence,
blame have been apportioned.
Until he is given a name.

END OF THE PEACH SEASON

The peaches are no longer in their prime:
Although their cheeks keep up a summer show,
They are living now on borrowed time.

To score with knives such beauty seems a crime;
But, underneath the skin, dark bruises show
The peaches are no longer in their prime.

Like dying wasps in grass who cannot climb,
The sun is losing altitude and shows
It is living now on borrowed time:

Pinched skins, with which streaked sunsets chime,
And wasp-bored wells of syrup go to show
The peaches are no longer in their prime.

Bud and blossom (*still life*) first; then slime
(*Memento mori*) ends their rose-hued show.
They are living now on borrowed time.

Scrape out the mould, the pockmarked heart of grime,
Expose the sallow tissue that will show
The peaches are no longer in their prime,
They are living now on borrowed time.

COMING OF AGE

What age would my parents have been on our excited day-trip
to the city when, during a bone-china lunch in the convent
parlour – served under the oily portrait of the haloed
founder – my wimpled aunt remarked that they would pass
for twenty?

> What I do know
> is how young
> my dying mother was.
>
> How difficult it became
> to recognise her
> in her final weeks.
>
> How – down to her black
> cancer-painted nails –
> she looked as though
>
> she had lived
> to be the oldest
> woman on earth,
>
> as if it would take
> an archaeologist
> to excavate her grave.
>
> How my aunt, despairing
> of the limitations
> of a walled-in life,

would revoke her order.
How my father's darkest
chapter would abruptly close.

How my sister, below
the age for admittance
to the wards,

was plied with goodies
in the hospital shop:
all the chocolate

she could cope with,
all the fizzy orange
she could drink.

TO LOVE

the dead woman
in the living girl.
The child in the woman.
The tree planed
against its grain
into a coffee table.
The blossom in
the inner chamber
of the crab apple's heart.
To love the squawking
baby bird underpinning
the full-spanned hawk
and the silk purse
of piglet skin
stashed in the jute
sack of the sow.
The meadow grass
taking root
in the tarred car park.
The wolf howling
through the chimney
of the mongrel's throat.
The race memory
of unfenced space
agitating the battery hen.
The ancestral ape
in the chauffeur-driven
man with diplomatic plates.
Even the flu virus
which lays you low

but has its own
agenda to pursue,
like moss in paving slabs,
cracks in frescoes,
incinerator sparks.

SNAIL'S PACE

I look down on the snail as on a container ship
seen from a plane, its slow pace an illusion
caused by distance, filigree silver wash a ruff
of sea spray. It is on its way, no doubt, to feed
off my garden, cold mucous mouth watering at the thought
of a sweet-and-sour meal of compost, leaves.

I raise a foot, needing to hear a shell's crunch,
a squelch against cement. Or I might nip inside
for salt to liquidate it, watch the textured stretch-
fabric flesh fizz into extinction; no one is sentimental
towards snails, oozing as though squeezed from a rusty tube.
Yet I let it go about its sluggish routines in the end.

The horns scout like a ship's antennae, ready
to warn but pointless when faced with aerial attacks.
I even know the damp ivy-clad segment of the back wall
where it skulks on dry days, lurking in its chestnut shell,
sticky with phlegmatic glue; and though sometimes I reach
     over,
prise it off to teach it who is boss, I can never quite rise

to the callousness required to play God with its life.

VOTIVE CANDLES

Burning candles toast
a corner of the church:

To your good health,
happiness, success . . .

One lighting the next
like a nervous

chain smoker's cigarette:
little rockets, boosters,

launched to heaven,
knuckle-white with pleading.

When they gutter,
stutter, dwindle, taper off,

what is left
of inflamed hopes

is a hard waxen mass,
a host;

the shard of soap
with which

God washes
His spotless hands.

A STATION

after Jenő Dsida

An official announcement crackling like deep-fried fat
that our branch-line train would be three hours delayed.
A garbled explanation, some reference to points failure.

And so this Thursday night, I stamp feet on the platform's
    pier,
venturing to the edge of choppy dark, like a man walking
    a plank.
Back in the yellow, dank, retch-smelling station building,

I read maps cracked on walls, see pierced hearts squeezed
in felt-tip between names; a revving engine raises,
dashes hopes, abandoning me to loneliness again, a pattern

repeating like the taste of supper in my mouth, thoughts
of betrayal in my mind. The blood is faltering in my veins.
A pale man, slumped near the blinded ticket kiosk, eyes

the clock; a young woman, tightening her veil of silence,
looks aside – it would be good to hear companionable sounds.
No chance. I listen as my inner demons prophecy what cruxes

lie in wait. Telegraph scaffolds line embankments.
Peter could snooze until cock-crow. James drools into
the neat pillow he has made of his scarf. John,

sleeping rough on concrete, keeps watch on his bad dreams.
Restless, I resume my platform vigil, fear streaming down
my forehead in the signal light's unyielding red.

Then, like switching tracks, I start to pray that my train
might never arrive, that my journey be indefinitely delayed,
my forward connections missed, that my cup might pass from me.

TOMORROW

Tomorrow I will start to be happy.
The morning will light up like a celebratory cigar.
Sunbeams sprawling on the lawn will set
dew sparkling like a cut-glass tumbler of champagne.
Today will end the worst phase of my life.

I will put my shapeless days behind me,
fencing off the past, as a golden rind
of sand parts slipshod sea from solid land.
It is tomorrow I want to look back on, not today.
Tomorrow I start to be happy; today is almost yesterday.

II

Australia, how wise you are to get the day
over and done with first, out of the way.
You have eaten the fruit of knowledge, while
we are dithering about which main course to choose.
How liberated you must feel, how free from doubt:

the rise and fall of stocks, today's closing prices
are revealed to you before our bidding has begun.
Australia, you can gather in your accident statistics
like a harvest while our roads still have hours to kill.
When we are in the dark, you have sagely seen the light.

III

Cagily, presumptuously, I dare to write 2018.
A date without character or tone. 2018.
A year without interest rates or mean daily temperature.
Its hit songs have yet to be written, its new-year
babies yet to be induced, its truces to be signed.

Much too far off for prophecy, though one hazards
a tentative guess – a so-so year most likely,
vague in retrospect, fizzling out with the usual
end-of-season sales; everything slashed:
your last chance to salvage something of its style.

HAY BARN

Riches of hay, hoarded
away in the barn, a cache
stuffed under a mattress,

were withdrawn over
winter, wads forked out
from a frosty cart.

Loose clumps
poked from smoking
mouths of cattle

who itched long
alligator chins
on wattle posts.

Though ransacked,
whittled down,
the hay smelt yet

of dusty summer,
of the beehive domes
swept dreamily home

on a horse-drawn float,
listing, hem brushing
against the uneven field,

sides ripping on thorns,
losing wisps to
a hedge-congested lane;

then unclasped, uncorseted
from twine bindings,
added to the stockpile

with sweaty, shirtless heaves
of men relieved
to have crammed each cavity

before the rodent-patter
of rain, creating a sanctuary
again, love nest,

escape hatch
for brooding hens
with dung-speckled eggs.

Ruminate on abundance
there some Sunday
after Mass,

still in your suit,
rooted to the ground
with awe.

NEWGRANGE

in memory of Miroslav Holub

They waited.
        They waited in vain.
                — HOLUB, 'The Earliest Angels'

I

Light scans the megalith on the winter solstice,
nosing forward, sniffing its way into the chambers,
twitching its rays like the whiskers of a laboratory rat.

It confronts the dark like white armies of lymphocytes.
It coats the walls like cholesterol on a middle-aged aortic
    arch.
Its glow is a 4 a.m. hospital corridor, a barium x-ray picture.

II

When you visited Newgrange — an off-colour autumn day —
you were seven minutes late: five thousand years
and seven minutes too late for admission;

so, you were refused access to the tomb, which loomed
before you like a time-operated safe; the tour guide,
a centurion, stood guard at the carved entrance stone.

III

Though you had no scientific means by which to predict this,
you were four years, nine months too early for the tomb,
where now you chart the frequency of light

at the tunnel's end and formulate a chaos theory
based on the flap of an angel's wing,
the velocity required for taking death by storm.

INTERIM REPORTS

for Teri Garvey

I

That precious time in bed
just before you rise for work.
Every second counts.
You live each minute
as though it were your last.

II

The formica tables
        and plastic chairs
of station cafés,
        roadside diners,
staff canteens;
        of hospitals where
relatives nurse
        styrofoam cups,
waiting for word
        to be conveyed
down tinned–salmon
        pink corridors.

III

A long illness bravely borne.
Words that crop up in obituaries.

The stress on every syllable
in its euphonious phrase.

IV

How are things?
How are you keeping?

How's the world
treating you?

Are you having
a nice day?

Have I caught you
at a bad moment?

How soon do you expect
to know for sure?

Should I ring back when
you're more composed?

V

Thank God for morphine
where pain management is concerned –

though, granted, it can have some side effects
(vertigo, facial flushing, bradycardia, palpitations,
vomiting, constipation, confusion, drowsiness, nausea,
sweating, orthostatic hypotension, hypothermia, restlessness,

mood swings, dry mouth, miosis, micturition difficulties,
ureteric or biliary spasm, raised intracranial pressure).

VI

When someone first asks of you
'Is he/she still alive?'
you will be well
into injury time.

VII

And where does the suffering go?
Down the hatch of the dialysis machine?
Ejected with a colostomy bag's waste?
Does it leave a flesh wound on raw innards,
notch the heart like a furrowed face?

Does it seep down, sweat and blood,
to the lower water table, or bubble up
like methane from a smothered mass grave
where an underground stream surfaces
through porous rock, a running sore?

VIII

The whisper of the word 'hospice'.
The hush at its heart.
The sedated body laid out on starched sheets.
The soul billowing on puffed pillows.

IX

The sisters in the children's unit
    couldn't have been kinder.

The bereavement support group
    helped us come to terms.

X

He had a comfortable night,
    the nurse assured me.

Her body was no longer contorted;
    she looked like her old self.

I felt I could detect a smile,
    as if he recognised me.

Her breathing became laboured,
    I pressed the emergency bell.

It was impossible to believe
    this was the end.

We had some good times together
    in spite of everything.

DEADLINES

The suspense of hanging
      around for an arbitrary call,
passing the years until

you're summoned, pacing
      between walls without
a firm appointment:

Read a glossy magazine.
      Break the crossword code.
Sit it out in your office,

driven to distraction
      by the workload;
at home, restore the paint

a malicious nail has
      scarred your car with;
threaten lawyers' letters

on your noisy neighbours;
      study the small print
in the share prospectus.

Your time will come
      when it gets a minute,
refusing to be pinned down,

despatching you at whim
      with a mercifully sudden
heart attack, snapping your back

in a car accident, setting
        your nightwear alight
in a hotel inferno,

taking your memory away
        so that you can't quite
put a name on its blank face.

TOWARDS A CESARE PAVESE TITLE

(Verrà la Morte e Avrà i Tuoi Occhi)

Death will come and it will wear your eyes.

Death demands the handover of your eyes.

Death eyes you, stares you in the face.

Then death assumes the running of your eyes.

Death powders cheeks, shadows eyes.

Death would take the eyes out of your head.

Death will seize your assets, cut off your eye supply.

Death lashes out at your defenceless eyes.

You are up to your eyes in death.

Death takes after you, eyes the image of yours.

You would recognise death with your eyes shut.

Death will give you dagger glances, evil eyes.

Death makes eye contact at last.

Death will come and it will steal your looks.

9 A.M.

A metal clatter of shutters.
A shattering of the street's silence.
A turning of keys, an unbolting of doors.
A reversing of 'CLOSED' verdicts.
A striped sun-awning is goaded
from its lair by a long pole.
Mobile signs are placed strategically
on the kerb, the direction of arrows checked.
Blue security men, not yet on their guard,
step out for a smoke or breathe the light.
The gift boutique smells of buffed wax polish,
the cosmetics section atomises into perfumes.
Brasso revamps an estate agent's image.
Two tramps, disturbed in doorways, fold up blankets.
Jewellers unlock their strongroom stock of gold rings
and bracelets, slip them back into plush velvet displays.
Name-tagged assistants drip bagged coins into tills.
Flowers, bleary-eyed from all-night truck journeys,
revive in cool vases, open wide.
Dust is sucked by vacuum cleaners
or brushed aside, swept towards gutters.
A hairdresser assesses a fringe
of tepid water with her hand.
'The usual' for a bakery customer means
a roll and butter, a tea-break muffin.
Bacon, egg, sausage in a coffee shop.
A newspaper, a slice of toast.
9 o'clock and all goes well.
Everyone is present and correct.

FRIDAY

We are driving home.
Work is over, the weekend ours
        like a gift voucher
to spend as we feel inclined.

        We pass the armed guard
of whitethorn, the guard
        of honour of poplars,
until our favourite

        half-mile stretch
where a canopy of branches
        spans the road
like a triumphal arch.

        Our car tunnels into
this leafy underpass,
        entering its funnel,
its decompression chamber.

        Sheep are shearing fields;
lambs bound like woolly dogs
        just released from the leash.
We have squeezed through

        the filter of trees
and now, renewed, detoxified,
        we are on the downward
slope towards home.

ONLY

It is only skin.
It can be artificially cultured these days.

It is only breath.
As often sour as sweet.

It is only nerve tips.
Invariably sensational in response.

It is only lips, one on top of the other.
Shedding their unsavoury scales.

It is only warmth.
Everyone hovers around the 37° mark.

It is only hormones, emitting primitive signals.
Easily reproduced under laboratory conditions.

It is only blood.
The dilation can be clinically explained.

It is only a glandular reaction.
Nothing to get worked up about.

It is only desire.
An impulse inspired electrochemically.

It is only a fluttering heart.
It has a finite number of strikes.

It is only one organism among many.
A million clones could be arranged.

It is only that your moment has arrived.
It is only for now.

TO A LOVE POET

I

Fortysomething did you say? Or more?
By now, no one could care less either way.
When you swoop into a room, no heads turn,
no cheeks burn, no knowing glances are exchanged,

no eye contact is made. You are no longer
a meaningful contender in the passion stakes.
But a love poet must somehow make love,
if only to language, fondling its contours,

dressing it in slinky tropes, caressing
its letters with the tongue, glimpsing it darkly
as though through a crackling black stocking
or a chiffon blouse, arousing its interest,

varying the rhythm, playing speech against
stanza like leather against skin, stroking words
wistfully, chatting them up, curling fingers
around their long fair declensions of hair.

II

Never again, though, will a living Muse
choose you from the crowd in some romantic city –
Paris, Prague – singling you out, her pouting lips
a fountain where you resuscitate your art.

Not with you in view will she hold court to her mirror,
matching this halter-neck with that skirt, changing her mind,
testing other options, hovering between a cashmere
and velvet combination or plain t-shirt and jeans,

watching the clock, listening for the intercom or phone.
Not for your eyes her foam bath, her hot wax, her hook-
     snapped
lace, her face creams, moisturisers, streaks and highlights.
Not for your ears the excited shriek of her zip.

Look to the dictionary as a sex manual.
Tease beauty's features into words that will assuage
the pain, converting you – in this hour of need –
to someone slim and lithe and young and eligible for love
     again.

LIFE CYCLE

in memory of George Mackay Brown

January. Wind bellows. Stars hiss like smithy sparks.
The moon a snowball frozen in mid-flight.
George is rocking on his fireside chair.

February. The sea loud at the end of the street.
Ferries cancelled. Snowdrops seep through dampness.
George is sitting down to mutton broth.

March. Oystercatcher piping. Early tattie planting.
Gull-protected fishing boats wary of the equinoctial gales.
George is tired by now of his captivity.

April. Cloud boulders roll back from the Easter sun.
The tinker horse, a cuckoo, in the farmer's field.
George is taking the spring air on Brinkie's Brae.

May. Scissors-tailed swallows cut the tape, declare summer open.
A stray daddy-long-legs, unsteady on its feet as a new foal.
George is sampling home-brew from his vat.

June. Butterfly wings like ornamental shutters. Day scorches
down to diamonds, rubies before being lost at sea.
George is picnicking with friends on Rackwick beach.

July. Another wide-eyed sun. Its gold slick pours like oil
on the untroubled waves. Shoppers dab brows as they gossip.
George is drafting poems in a bottle-green shade.

August. Pudgy bees in romper suits suckled by flowers.
Well water rationed. Trout gills barely splashed.
George is hiding from the tourists' knock.

September. A brace of wrapped haddocks on the doorstep.
Mushrooms, snapped off under grass tufts, melt in the pan.
George is stocking up his shed with coal and peat.

October. Porridge and clapshot weather. Swan arrivals,
    divers.
Sun hangs, a smoking ham, suspended in the misty air.
George is ordering a hot dram at the pub.

November. Rain shaken out sideways like salt. Hail pebbles
flung against the window to announce winter's return.
George is adding a wool layer to his clothes.

December. Three strangers, bearing gifts, enquire the way
to byre and bairn. A brightness absent from the map of stars.
George's craft is grounded among kirkyard rocks.

DELEGATES

Today, we have no responsibility for the world.
We are in transit between airport lounges.
It is Tuesday in one jurisdiction, Monday in another.
We cannot be tied down, we are on the run like fugitives,
sheltered by date lines and time zones, escaping tax
regulations, weather alerts, dodging the present tense.

*

Container boats – ferrying
imports, exports – can be
seen from our mezzanine.

A backdrop to negotiations
like a painted seascape
framed on an office wall,

turned to when minds wander
or memories are rifled
for near-precedents.

*

A strategic break. Mass migration towards the wash room.
A lemon squirt from your shrivelled member, then out again
to drum up support for your proposal: hands, perfumed
with liquid soap, gesture as you outline your rationale.

*

Always a harried official,
plastic ballpoint in mouth
like a thermometer, checking
the viability of a draft
beginning with the words,
'Notwithstanding the provisions of . . .'

*

An end–of–term mood
in the July conference rooms:
microphones switched off,
booth lights dimmed,
the open spaces
of the corridors
thinned of population,
attachés pressing '01'
in the mirrored lifts,
interpreters returning
to their mother tongues.

*

Friday night delays
of flights to capitals
by national carriers,
the wait for take-off clearance.

Jackets folded, stowed with duty-free,
balding heads lie back,
soak up news distributed
by smiling cabin crews.

*

Rushing the glass
      arrivals door,
you pick your
      expectant daughter
from the throng,
      playschool painting
elevated at the barrier
      like a name-board.

BUYING A LETTERBOX

Another mouth to feed.
Our best face
turned to the world,
catching the brass
eye of the sun.

Should we buy the type
that snaps shut,
a trap scattering
bills and final reminders
like feathers, fur?

Or the limper kind
that yields easily,
tongue slobbering around
the postman's hand,
yet still eats anything,

digesting the bad news
as casually as the good?

WEATHER PERMITTING

I

The August day you wake to takes you by surprise.
Its bitterness. Black sullen clouds. Brackish downpour.
A drift-net of wetness enmeshes the rented cottage,
towels and children's swimwear sodden on the line.

Dry-gulleted drains gulp down neat rain.
Drops bounce from a leaking gutter with hard,
uncompromising slaps: and, like resignation
in the face of death, you contemplate winter

with something close to tenderness, the sprint
from fuel shed to back door, the leisurely
ascent of peat smoke, even the suburban haze
of radiator flues when thermostats are set.

You warm to those thoughts as you sit there,
brainstorming ways to keep the family amused,
plans abandoned for barefoot games on dry sand.
Handcraft shops? Slot-machine arcades? Hotel grills?

In truth – manipulating toast crumbs backwards,
forwards at the unsteady table's edge – you'd prefer
to return to your bed as if with some mild
ailment, pampered by duvet, whiskey, cloves.

II

Let it rain.
Let the clouds discharge their contents like reserve tanks.
Let the worms burrow their way to the topsoil
from whatever dank Sargasso they were spawned in.
Let dampness rot the coffin-boards of the summer house.
Let the shrubs lose their foothold in the wind,
the nettles lose their edge, the drenched rat
with slicked-back hair scuttle to its sewage pipe.
Let the tropical expanses of the rhubarb leaves
serve as an artificial pond, a reservoir.
Let the downpour's impact on the toolshed be akin
to the dull applause on an archive recording of a love duet.
Let the bricklayers at the building site wrap
pathetic sheets of polythene around doomed foundations.
Let the limb ripped from the tree's socket
hover fleetingly in the air, an olive branch.
Let a rainbow's fantail unfurl like a bird of paradise.
Let a covenant be sealed, its wording watertight.
Let the floods recede.
Let there be light.

III   *after Leopardi*

The storm runs out of wind; nature, which
abhors a silence, fills the vacancy with birdsong.
Deserting the airless, low-ceilinged coop,
the hen repeats herself ad infinitum. Replenished
like the rain-barrels, hearts grow sanguine.

Hammering resumes. Humming. Gossip. Croons.
Sun strides down lanes that grass has repossessed,
takes a shine to the brasses at the hotel where,
by the window she thrust open, the chambermaid
is marvelling at the cleansed freshness, calm.

Balm of mind and body. Will we ever feel
more reconciled to life than now, ever
know a moment more conducive to new hopes,
eager beginnings, auspicious starts?
How easily pleased we are. Rescind

the threat of torment for the briefest
second and we blot out dark nights of the soul
when lightning flashes fanned by wind
ignited fire and brimstone visions.
Sorrow is perennial; happiness, a rare

bloom, perfumes the air – so that we breathe
with the ease of a camphor-scented chest
from which congestion has just lifted.
Lack of woe equates with rapture then,
though not till death will pain take full leave

of our senses, grant us permanent relief.

BREVIARY

Departures

He has made up his mind.
He is on his way,
in a mud-stained trench-coat,
five days' stubble.

To judge by his bag,
he is determined to stay.
His knock on your door
will mean trouble.

Real trouble.

Web Site

Silk stretched out
     like a retractable tape,
taking the measure
     of the leafy site.
Planet's guyropes.
     Latitude. Longitude.
The world dangling
     by a thread.

Three-month Sabbatical

Three lambs that are mine to rear by hand.
Three mythic islands springing up. Three brass bands.
Three voyages. Three visions. Three promised lands.

Jack

    The longer he is dead
the less our memories are eclipsed
    by that bald-moon look his friends
could not identify him with.

    His hair begins to grow,
his beard will need a trim.
    We are nearly back
on speaking terms with him.

Edward Hopper

Everything in Silbers Pharmacy has become redundant:
gravid flasks of watercolour fluid cracked,
doors softened into rot, dispensing drawers
and hardwood counters sold to dealers as a job lot.

Patent cures were superseded like the archaic *Pharmacy*
on the fascia, mutant diseases succeeding one another
as a new century outmanoeuvres an old. The image alone
stays immune, conserved in varnish like formaldehyde.

PART TWO

CHURCHYARD VIEW: The New Estate

Taking it all with us,
we move in.

*

On their side, inviolable silence.
On ours, hammering, pounding,
sawing, clawing out foundations
with the frenzy of someone buried alive.

*

We like our dead well-seasoned.
Newly-ground soil disturbs.

*

She could wind him round her little finger
that is now solid bone.

*

My halogen light with sensor
alert for resurrections.

*

Every crow suspected as a raven,
every pigeon inspected for vulturehood.

*

They mark their death-days among themselves,
bake a mud cake, make candles of wax fingers.

*

Young since they were born.
Young since they were teenagers.
Young since they staged a coming-of-age
bash in the tennis club hall.
Young since they played non-stop
basketball for charity sponsorship.
This being young could only go on for so long.

*

Our houses, giant mausoleums,
dwarf their tombs to kennels.

*

Crab-apple windfalls
at the cemetery wall
no one collects for jelly.

*

The churchyard in shadow
like a north-facing garden.

*

Our freehold title
when the mortgage is redeemed.
Their graves to be maintained
perpetually by bequests.

*

Call my wrong number
in the small hours of the night.
Remind me how bad
things might – will – be.

*

A lip–puffed, ear–blocked, glow–nosed
head cold is what they feel nostalgia for.

*

How much it took to sustain their lives:
heaps of gravel, travel coupons, steel pads,
roll–on deodorants, bran flakes, tampons.

*

The dead seem more at ease in autumn
as the time to hibernate comes near.

*

Written before they were born,
these books foretold
anxiety and strife and war.
And yet they were born.

*

In our pine bed, we hear them stirring
when floorboards creak, pipes cheep.

*

The prehensile clasp of the dead
grasping at prayer books
with straw-yellow claws.

*

Most die over a lifetime;
others die all at once, missing in action.

*

Not a footprint dipped in churchyard snow.

*

The child's coffin
like a violin case.
A pitch which parents' ears
can hear through clay.

*

Buried talents lie.
Hoards unexcavated by posterity.

*

Scan the obit columns, uniform as war graves.
Check the maiden names, the regretting children.
Whole cities and towns wiped out.
A plague on all your houses.

*

A hearse in rush-hour traffic:
a ghost at the feast.

*

Two sisters
who wished each other dead
languish side by side.

*

Plots divided like vegetable allotments.

*

All behind them now.
The blushed fumblings of sex.
Interventional radiology.
Expense account lunches.
Games of bridge.

*

Death is the aftertaste of life.

*

Those who fester better than others.
Those who manage it more neatly.
Those fussy about the order
in which their organs decompose.
Those who discover an aptitude for death
they never had for life.

*

The blackness of
the cemetery blackbird,
its song an octave lower.

*

Above prison-high walls,
the trees – up to their knees
in slaughter – protest their innocence
to the outside world.

*

Who had a crush on the girl
six headstones away.
Who couldn't muster
the courage.
Who wouldn't make
the first move.

Paupers' anonymous plots.
Families in layers like bunk beds.

Crypts where coffins rest
on shelves, left luggage.

The rusted, railed-off holdings
of those whose souls

appropriate a private
heaven for themselves.

*

Add the total suffering of these bodies.
Deduct their combined pleasure.
What doth it profit a man?

*

As you were built on bone,
your house was built on sand.
Not a stone will stand upon stone.

A painted wall is a white lie.
You will crumble to the ground.
Your house will sicken, die.

*

I stare at the graves
like a sailor gazing out to sea.

*

A skull smashed,
        the crust of concrete
is sledgehammered open –
        dust to dust –
welcoming an addition
        to the family.

*

For whom growing pains, walking frames,
crash diets, price rises, self-esteem
were live issues once upon a time.

*

Days when death comes so close,
you say No to life.
Days when you could show death
how to live.

*

Should this end in spring
when death is overwhelmed
by winding sheets of green?
Or Halloween when
I overnight with friends?

PART THREE

FAMILY ALBUM

I

A rose window, buried
since Cromwellian times,
was unearthed in the henhouse
of a children's adventure story.
I read about it, waiting in the car
for my father, as a shivery evening
descended on the village like an Asian flu.

II

The empty Atrixo jar is what survives
of our mother's hands: hands that plumped pillows,
milked drinking water from the pump, spread suds
and beeswax polish through her children's lives.

III

Rained-out day-trips.
Vain buckets, spades.
        The beach like
        newly-laid concrete
where, growing boys,
we ached to build
        our castles
        in the healthy air.

July. My mother and I are in the kitchen.
Sun, outlined behind mist, swaggers into view.
Radio tuned to Athlone for the requests show,
she soaks the charred saucepan to which
a crust of porridge sticks, scrapes laval
streaks from a blue-rimmed egg-cup, squeezes
a plastic bottle for the last dregs of detergent.

I dry the dishes, leave her then, stuffing the gullet
of a circular washing machine with clothes,
adjusting the crank on the manual wringer.
Russian vine invades the outdoor toilet,
loose newspaper headlining scandals, crimes.
In my spongy sandals, I walk the cinder paths
between sweet and sharp competing fragrances.

Morning glories tighten their grip. Spurred nasturtiums.
Lettuce hearts harden. Beyond the hedge, bordered by silk
poppies – red slept-in party dresses – the dip and rise
of headscarfed women cycling on high nellies to the town.
Sound waves of conversation ripple through the heat.
Insects hum like chainsaws in a rain forest. Larks
about their business. A moist rubber-mouthed frog.

And snuff of dog roses. And wasps on house calls.
And a sudden outburst of church bells. And great
surges of silence. And my sister's skipping rhymes.
And berries roasting on their stalks, like fish grilled
on the bone. And a grasshopper's rhythms, a bamboo
thwacked by a bored child along park railings.
And permed dahlias. And days and days and days of this.

V

No work. No school.
        Sunday, January 20th 1963.
Wary cars are testing
        fresh clots of snow.
Crinkled seals of ice
        unbroken on the puddles,
rain-barrel frozen tight,
        what might our outlook hold
when the icicle sword
        guarding the bay window
corrodes and we gradually
        drift apart?

VI

The front door ajar: a black hole
through which a hurling commentary
curls, like smoke shavings off tar.
I play with my cousins in a trailer
lined with grain shot, locks of hay.

Free till milking, uncles in oaten socks
lean towards the radio from timber forms.
Later, hair brilliantined, Old Spice
and soap outflanking vapours of hot cow,
they will dash to the Sunday dance.

Calf mash bubbles in a cauldron
on the range. A hen, flapping with
hurt pride, is evicted from the kitchen.

The sun locates an opening in the clouds
to slip through, rendering things precious

for a second: our chubby, toad–like
Volkswagen; straw roof thatch; chunks
of turnip that spill, gold winnings,
from the mangler when my brother
shoulders the iron handle's strain.

VII

Here in the dream
my father clasps
my mother's hand.
Not a word is said.

And though they are both dead,
they have enough flesh left
to shoot a glance
at one another's eyes.

That look, I realise,
they always used
when transmitting secret knowledge
above their children's heads.

VIII

The crane, throwing its weight around,
jib pointed towards the future,

distracts me with a shade not seen
since primary school: gobstopper blue.

I suck the paintwork white
with greedy eyes.

Now the gobstopper becomes
a demolition ball:

hurled against the wailing
walls of childhood,

it starts to taste
of love and aniseed and fear.

IX

No exams this year.
The summer break is under way.
Days are brimful of potential.
My father takes me on his sales drive
to small towns near the county border.

Broad face cleared of thistle-spiky
bristle by a safety blade
– worked up to a lather
with shaving stick and brush –
he is glowing with good health,

glad of the company, the chat.
We overtake a bakery van, almost
able to catch the doughy draught of soft

white bread, cracked terracotta crusts
we'd love to pick holes in.

A milk churn on a donkey cart;
the farmer – legs dangled next
to an outsize orange wheel – salutes.
Hay-scented air streams through
our side-windows like thyme.

Fields are flourishing and abundant
or raked and baled and bound.
We laugh at the clapboard church
we pass but cross ourselves nonetheless.
Guess how many dogs we'll see

between here and Clogheen?
We each make a stab.
Dogs asleep in dung-scabbed farmyards.
Dogs lunging from boreens at our tyres.
Dogs hobbled to inhibit straying.

Down one steep, narrow-waisted road.
Up another.
Tracing the stout-walled perimeters
of a demesne; the disused railway line
an abandoned, meandering, flower-hemmed lane.

Council men with drippy cans of bitumen
stand in the shade between potholes.
He is so alive, my father, he can talk, drive,
become animated about a gymnastic stoat, the lacy
patterns sun stencils through the trees.

He smiles at some remark of mine.
Tonight, he will repeat it to my mother
as she fills the ringing tea pot
with hot water; and, dinner eaten, will
record it proudly in his diary like a sale.

X

Oranges were my exotic fruit
when young: gaudy leatherette
of skin, profuse sachets of juice.

Then peaches. I must have reached
eleven by the time of my first–hand
encounter with an uncanned peach,

pronouncing the ripe word to the grocer
who drew one from its nesting place,
laying it to rest in my disbelieving palm.

XI

Grey. The dishwater disgorged in anger against the kitchen
wall.

Grey. The cotton vests worn under home–knit jumpers,
a shield for chest colds, damp rooms, harm.

Grey. A fog of affection and alarm dense enough to isolate
you from the world.

Grey. The pipe smoke signalling peace when your father lit up.

Grey. The dust multiplying neatly on the venetian blinds after she had died.

Grey. Still the colour in which your dreams preserve that house.

Grey that could bud suddenly into day-glo picture books, American comics, love displays.

XII

A lashing wet February night. Cold jabs of wind.
I park my bike. Stark unholy rainwater rushes
down the gutters of my exposed nose.

What a miracle it would take to step back
into my leaky shoes and enter the bleak,
unheatable cathedral (mosaics of angels,

wings gold-tipped like nibs; statuesque Marys
sheltering beneath the cross's beams) with faith
as firm as mine was then; ending a retreat,

we elevated rosary beads and scapulars for blessing,
roused to 'Hail Queen of Heaven' at the organist's
first hint; incense like a whiff of paradise.

Then trailing the May procession on its petal-strewn route
through the seminary grounds, apple trees in blossom,
high schoolboy voices breaking into hymns. Women in veils

and Child of Mary gowns. Sodality banners. Papal flags.

80

XIII

No, maybe I won't opt for a liquorice whip
or a powdery flying saucer after all; I swap
my 6d coin, sporting a silver greyhound,
for a cream pie (enough pennies yet to buy
ten real-looking cigarettes at lunch-hour).

The upper crust of chocolate is flecked
with little coloured dots that give my tongue
a sandpapery feel, exactly like our cat's,
the goo underneath like chewy ice-cream
jammed into the sugary inlet of a cone.

Though I'm tempted to start from the flat
wafery bottom, squared out like graph paper,
I work down conscientiously from the top,
gapped teeth meeting no resistance.
I drag the pleasure out all the way to school.

XIV

Saturday morning, our father ferries us to town.
A pound of this, a scoop of that, from fragrant sacks
of seeds, pellets, phosphates, feeds in Sutton's yard.
A pair of brass hinges at Molloy's hardware.
The library's squeaky-clean linoleum for Enid Blyton's
Secret Seven, a doctor-and-nurse story for our mother,
our father wavering between two gory wars.

Salmon-coloured stamps licked into savings books.
The sweet, addictive smell of pulped sugar beet
wafting our way on a raft of factory steam.
Bills to pay for clothes we'd tried on appro.
Then back to the car, pulling faces at passers-by,
while our father eyes a rival's cabbage plants,
doused and counted into hundreds at the market.

A busker plays a tarnished trumpet. Hawkers gesture.
Capped men off country buses check used suits for thickness.
Half-heads, teaty bellies, hard-salt flanks, smoked streaky
grace Molony's bacon window . . . My brothers and I caffle,
tire, then face out racing clouds until the world begins
to spin – like when our father swings us to dizziness,
sets us down on the kitchen's unstable ground.

XV

The air is light
as sponge cake.

We speak
the silent

language of
laden plates,

second helpings,
topped-up glasses,

running-over
cups.

NOCTURNE

Time for sleep. Time for a nightcap of grave music,
a dark nocturne, a late quartet, a parting song,
bequeathed by the great dead in perpetuity.

I catch a glance sometimes of my own dead at the window,
those whose traits I share: thin as moths, as matchsticks,
they stare into the haven of the warm room, eyes ablaze.

It is Sunday a lifetime ago. A woman in a now-demolished
    house
sings *Michael, Row the Boat Ashore* as she sets down the
    bucket
with its smooth folds of drinking water . . .

The steadfast harvest moon out there, entangled in the
    willow's
stringy hair, directs me home like T'ao Ch'ien: *A caged bird
pines for its first forest, a salmon thirsts for its stream.*

Some Recent Poetry from Anvil

Oliver Bernard
Verse &c.

Nina Bogin
The Winter Orchards

Heather Buck
Waiting for the Ferry

Nina Cassian
Take My Word for It

Peter Dale
Edge to Edge
SELECTED POEMS

Dick Davis
Touchwood

Carol Ann Duffy
The World's Wife
LIMITED EDITION

Time's Tidings (ed.)
GREETING THE 21ST CENTURY

Martina Evans
All Alcoholics Are Charmers

Michael Hamburger
Collected Poems 1941–1994
Intersections
Late

James Harpur
Oracle Bones